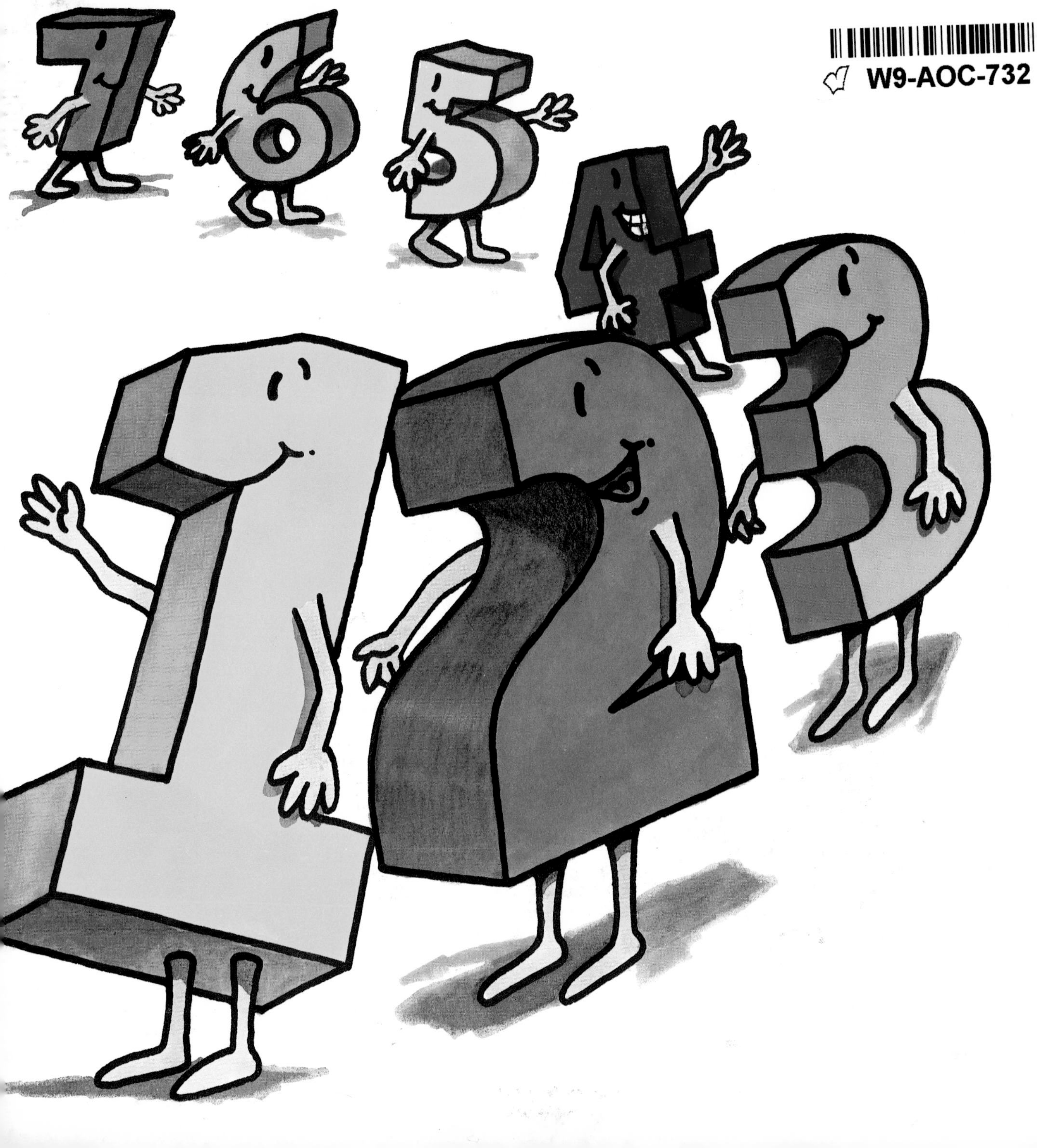

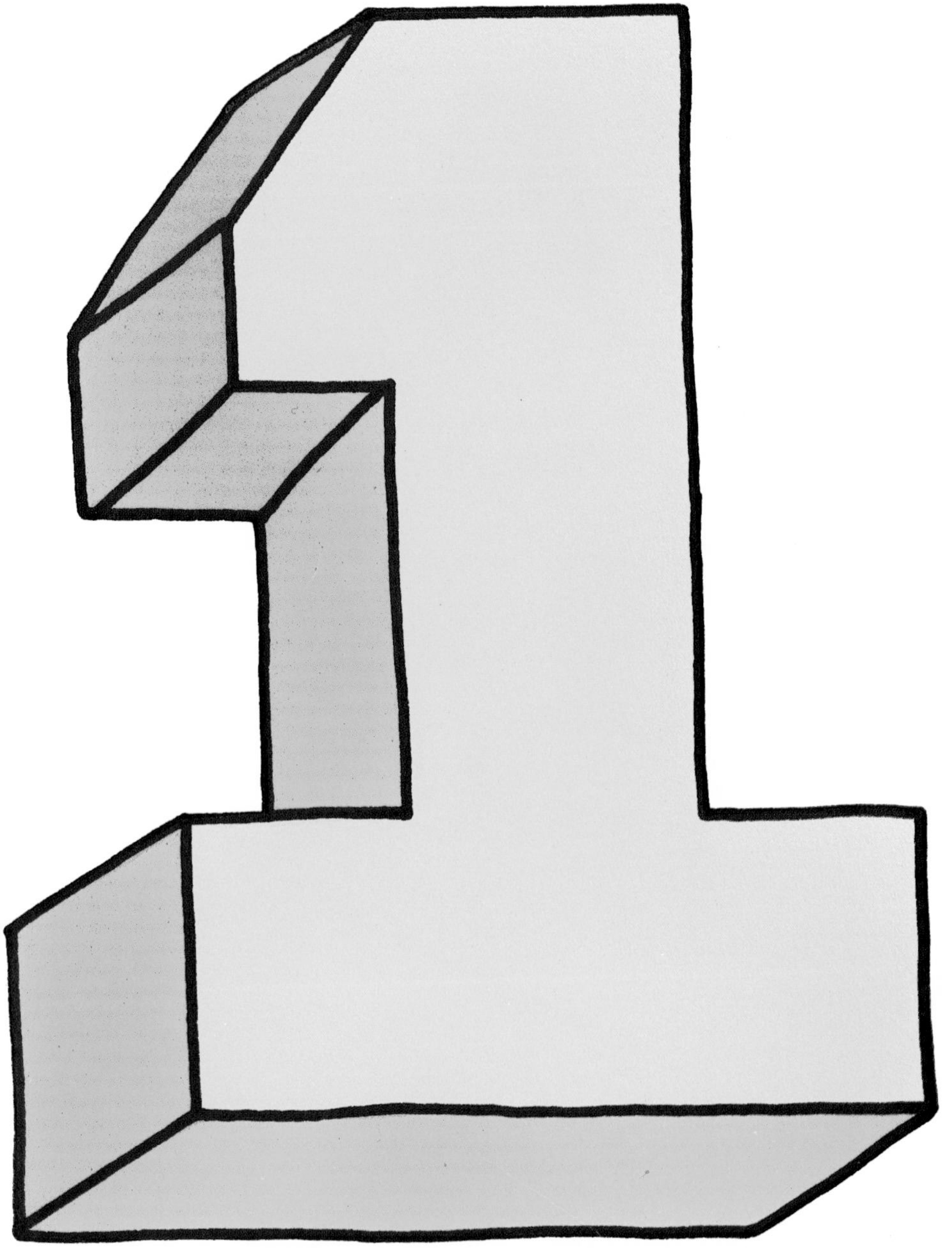

Dog

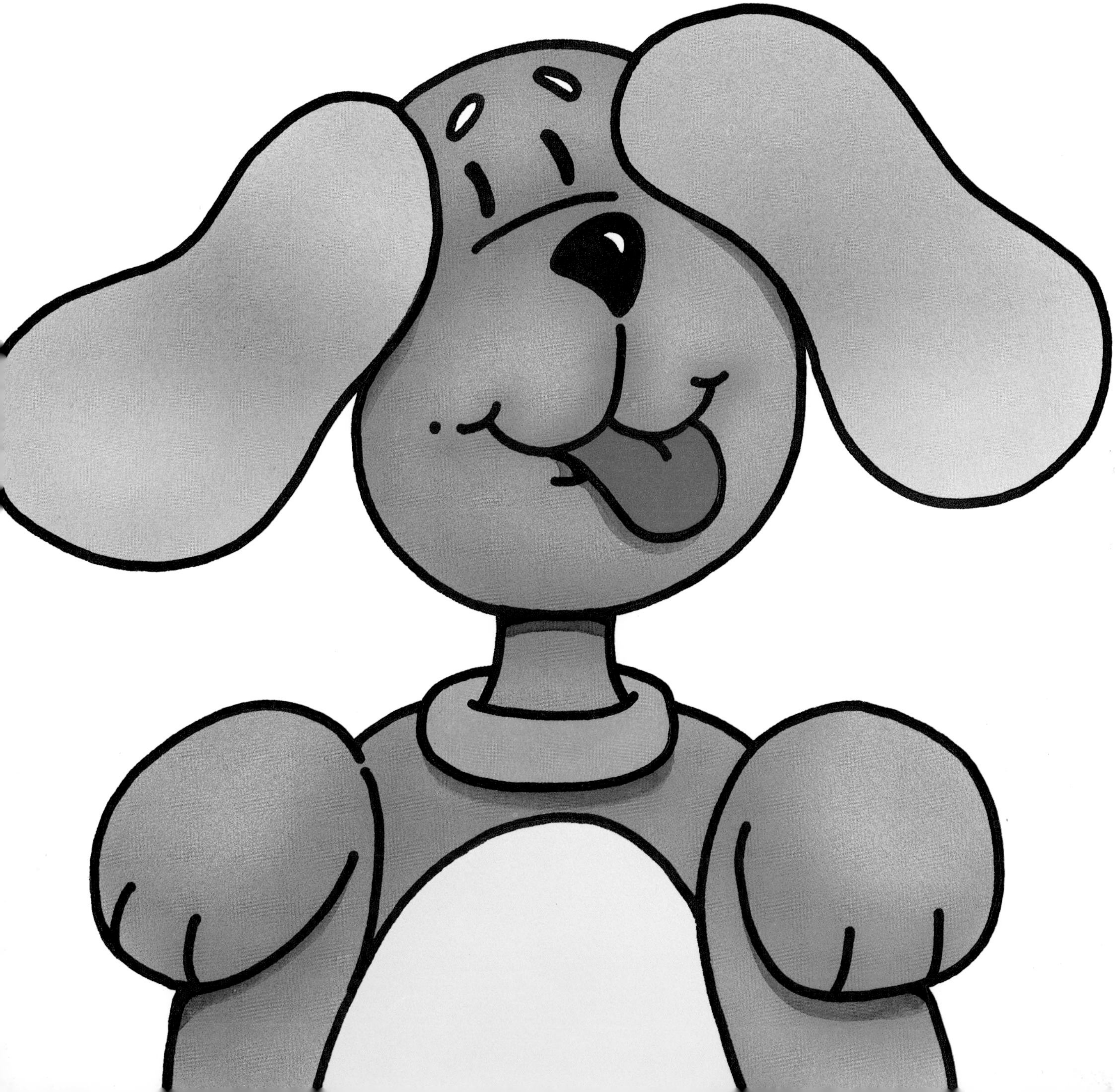

2 Birds

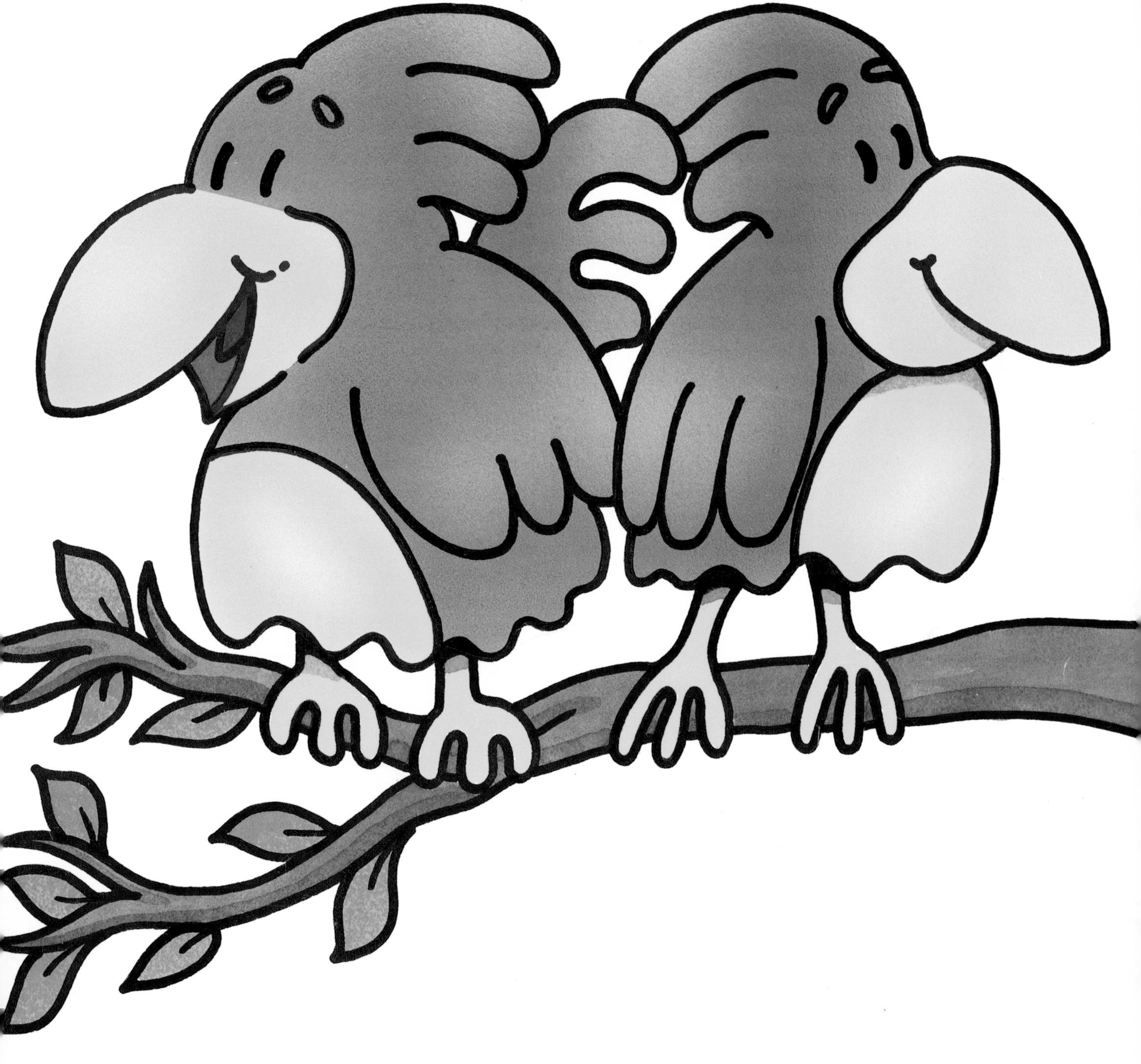

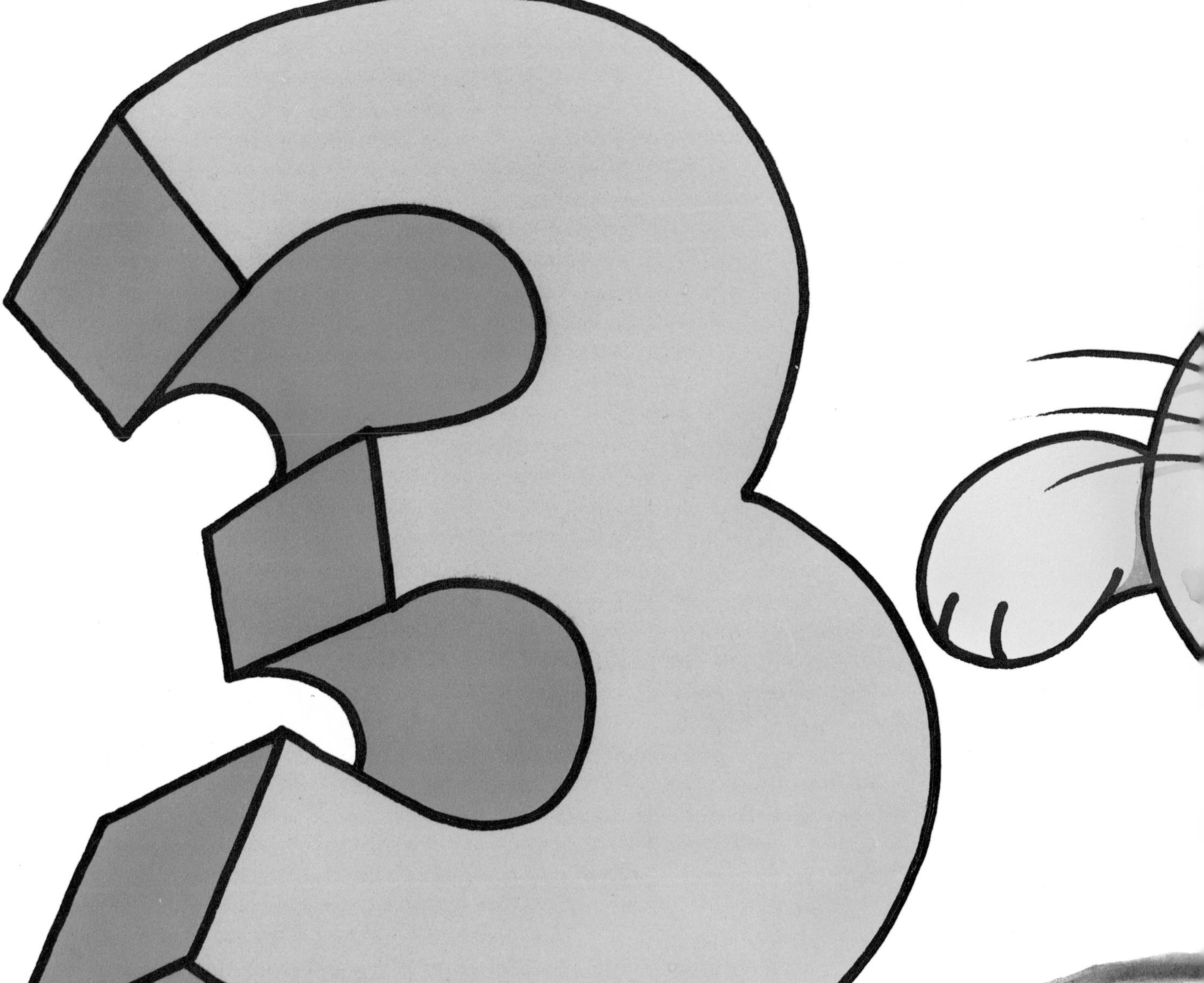

Cats

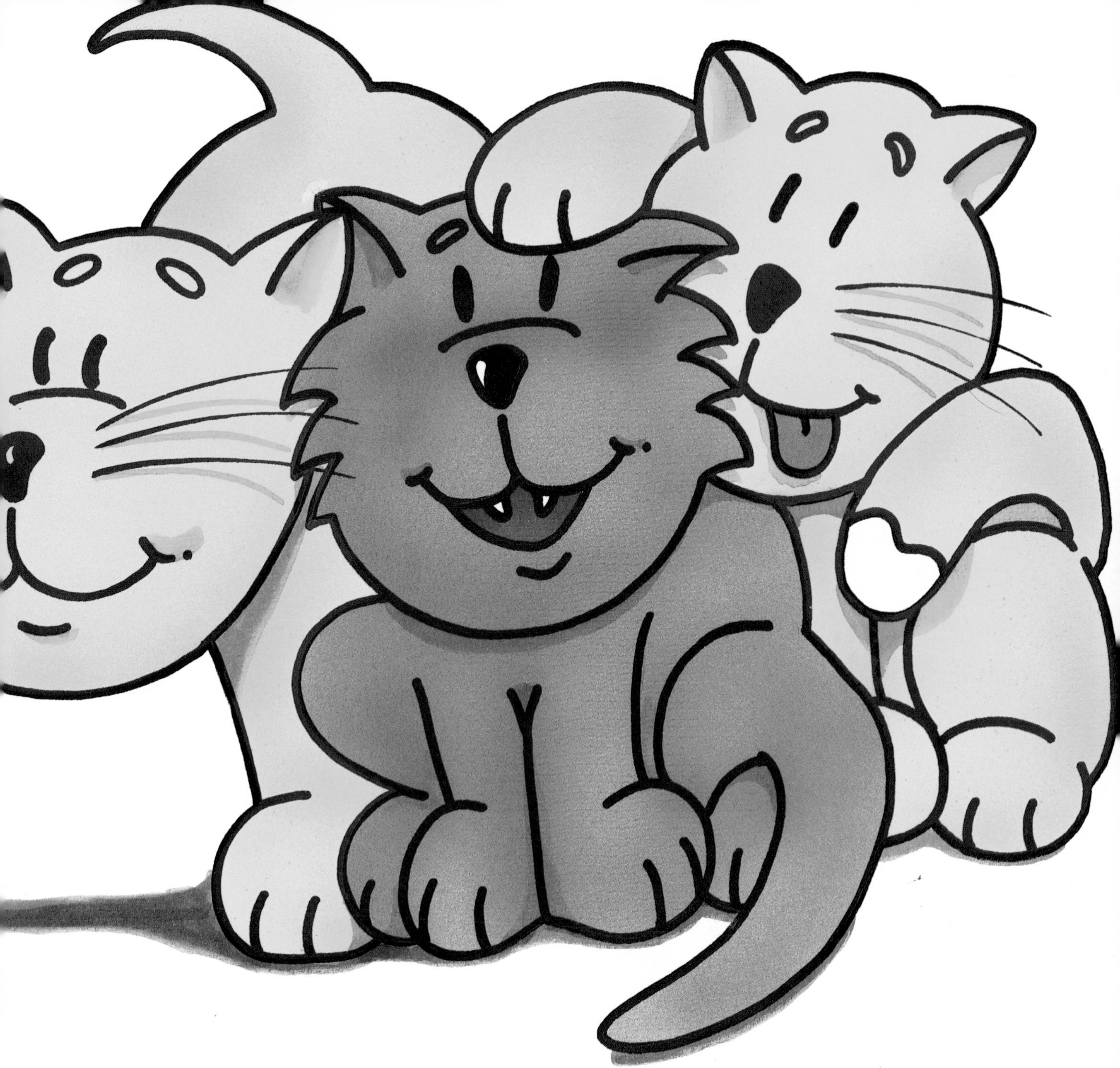

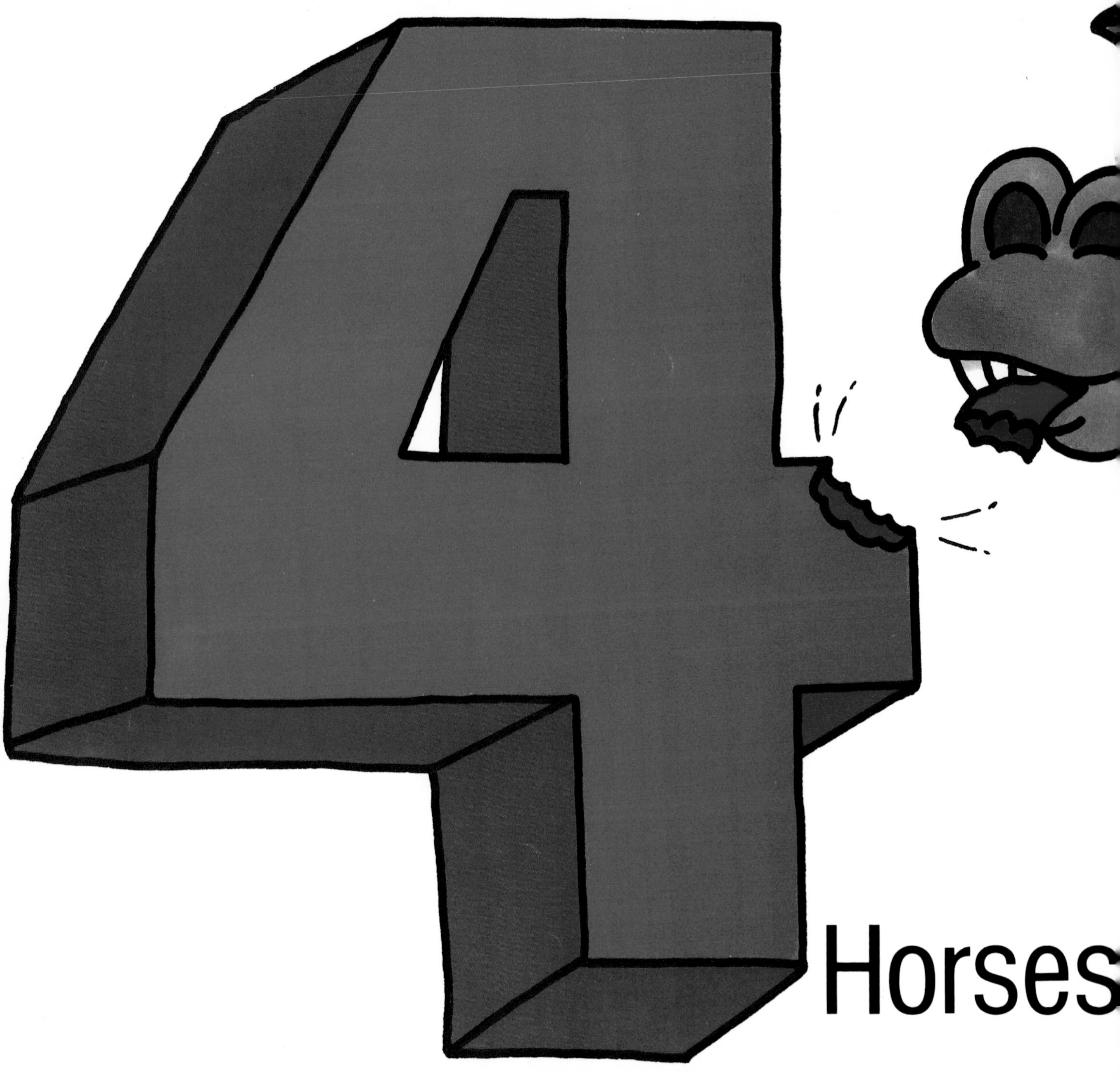

4 Horses

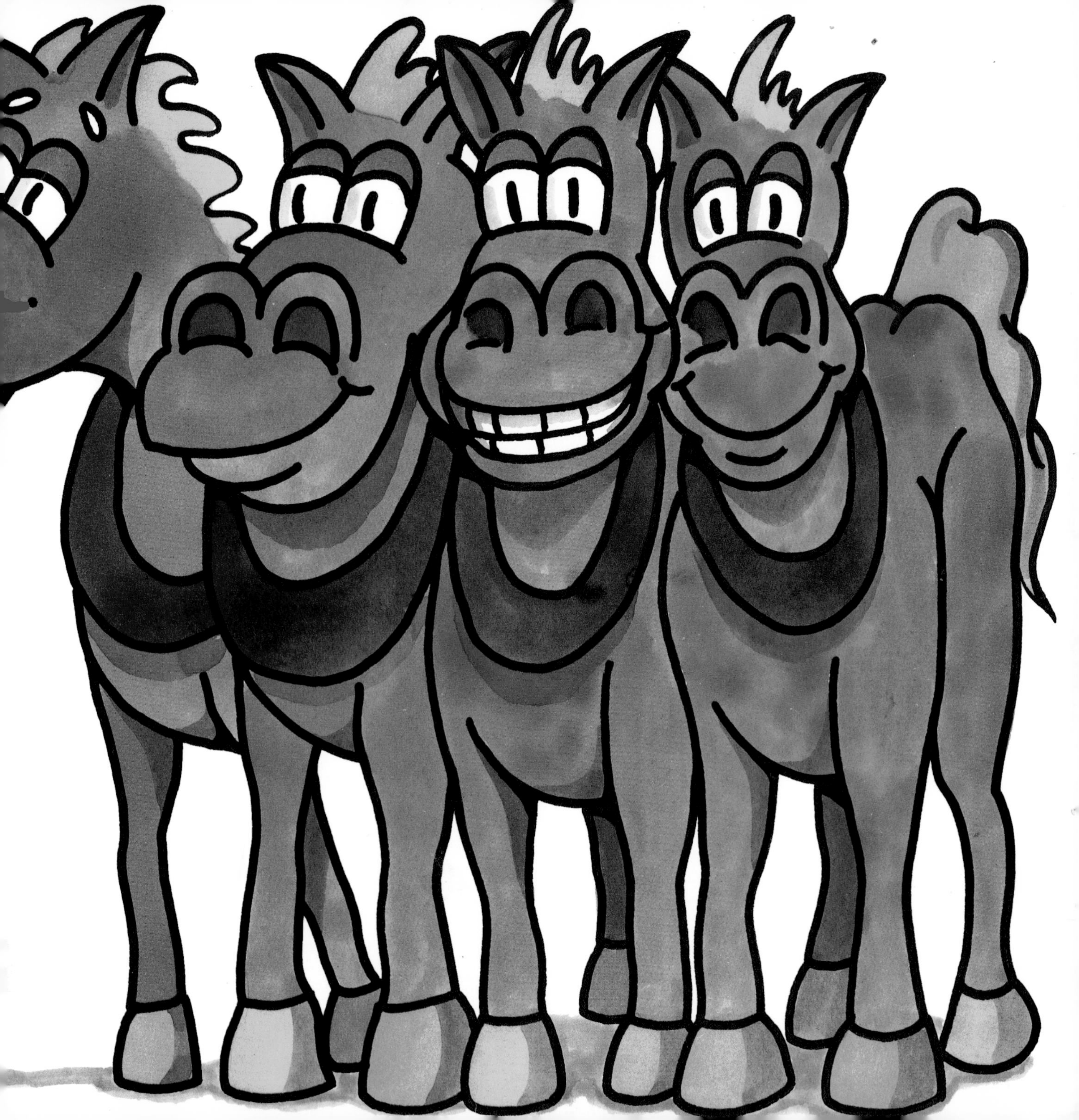

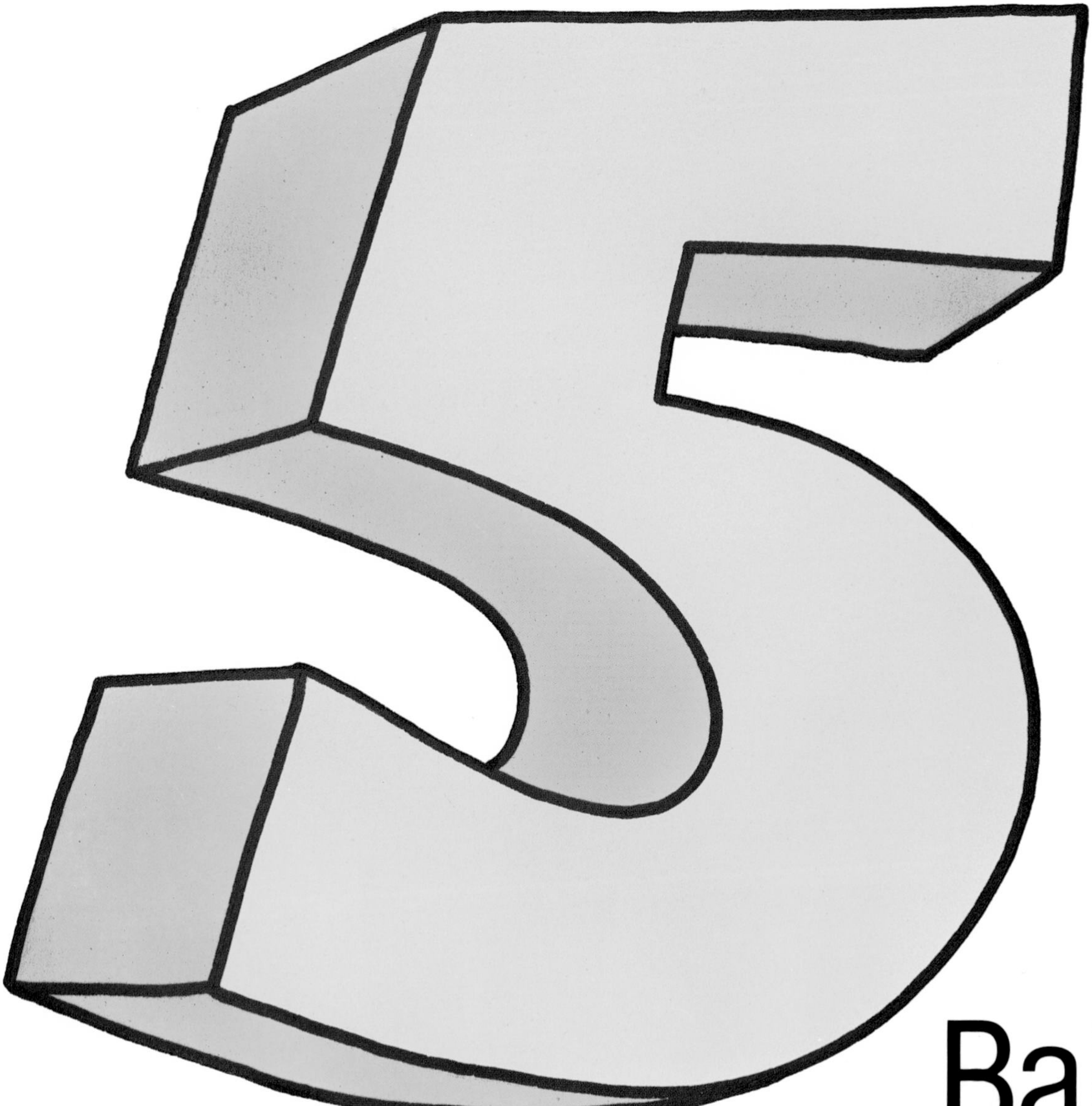

Babies

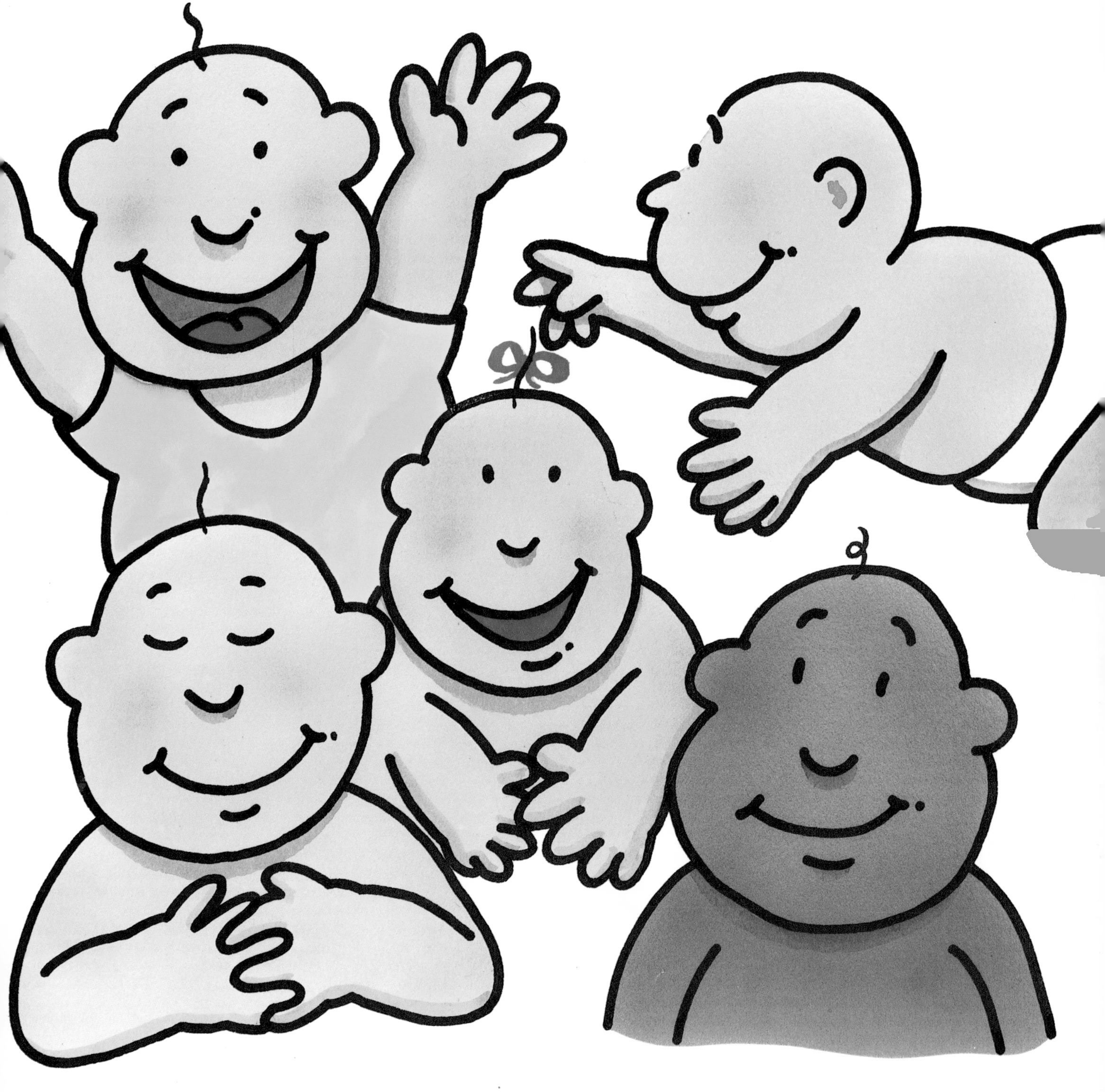

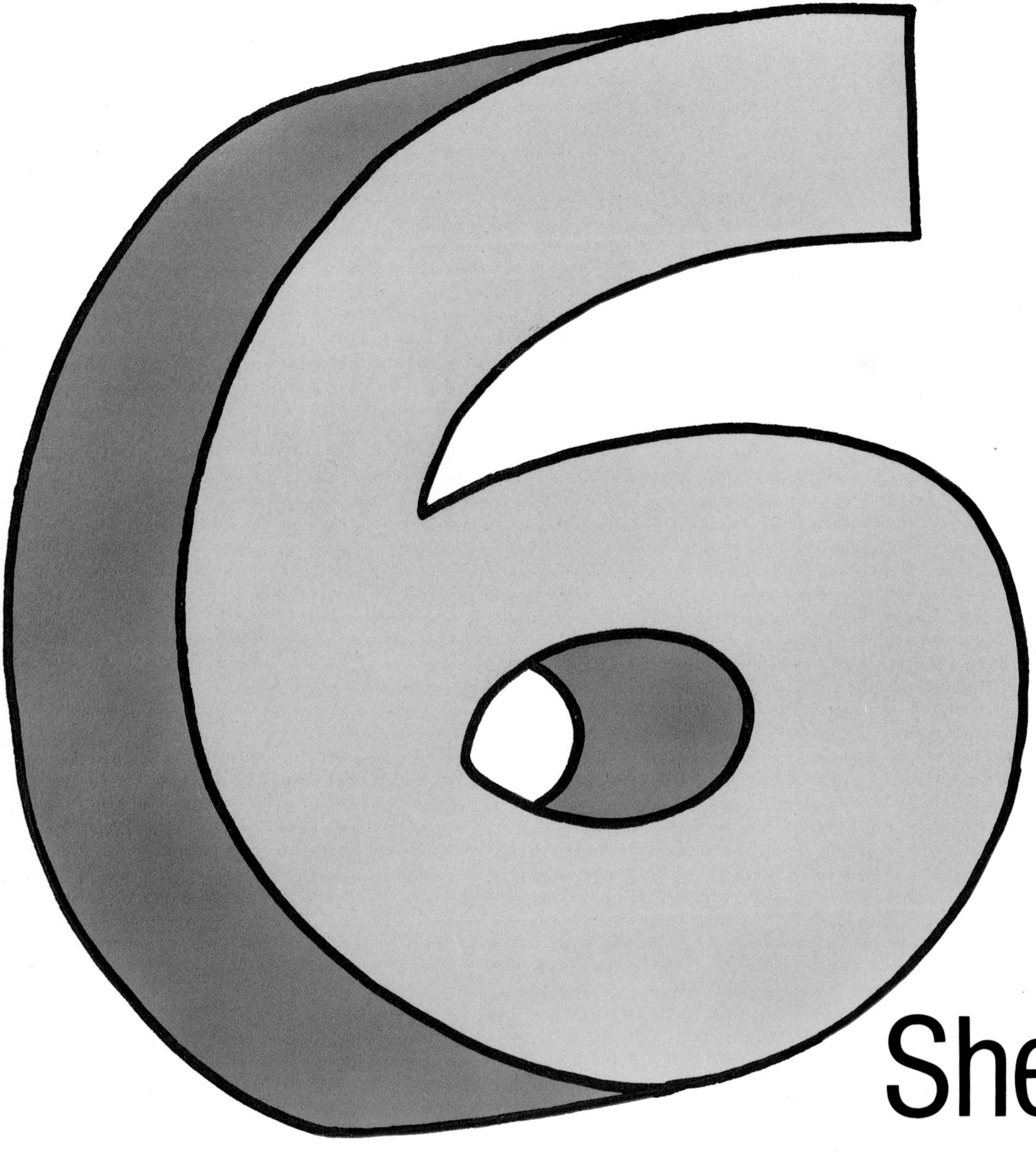

Sheep

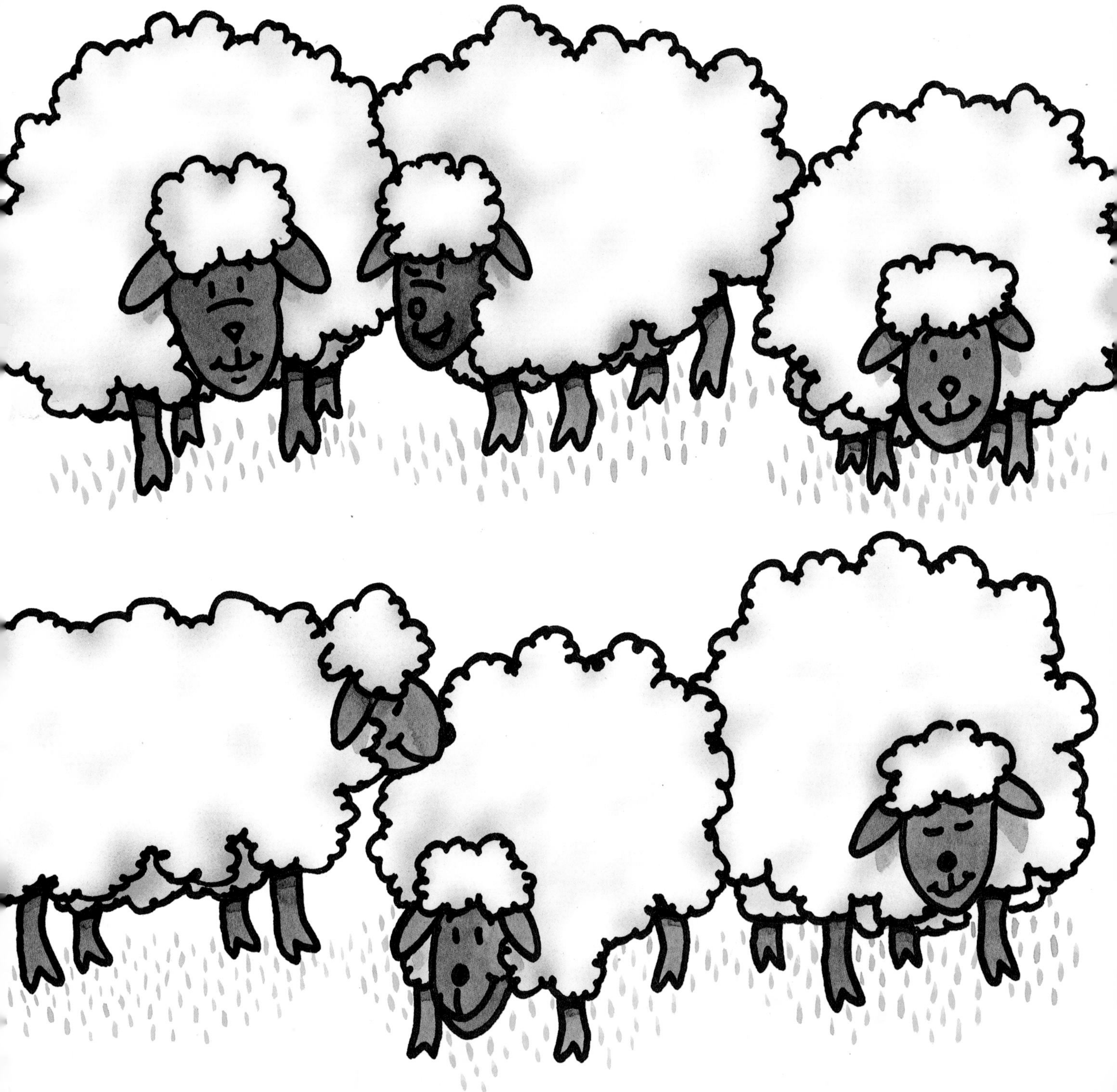

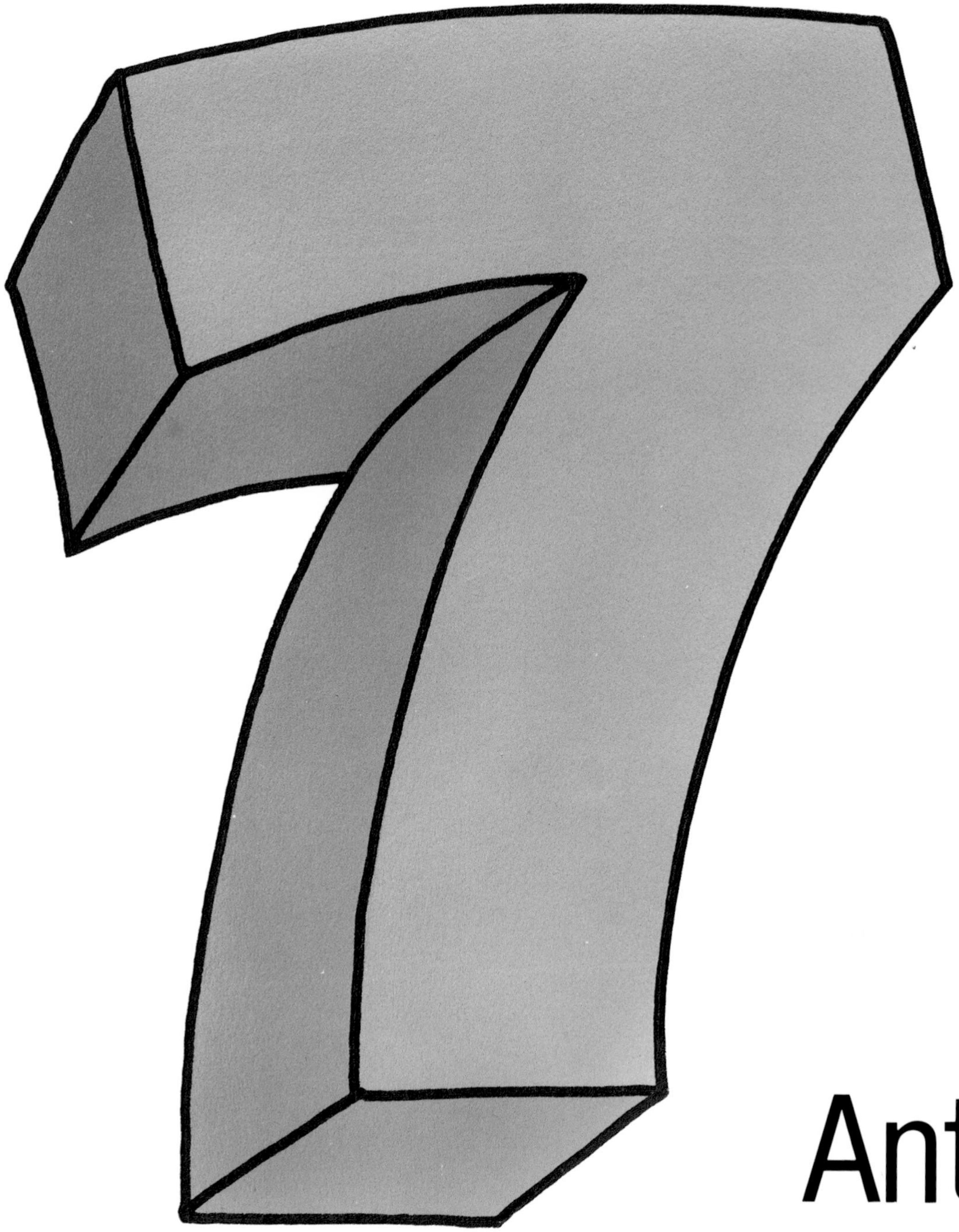

Ants

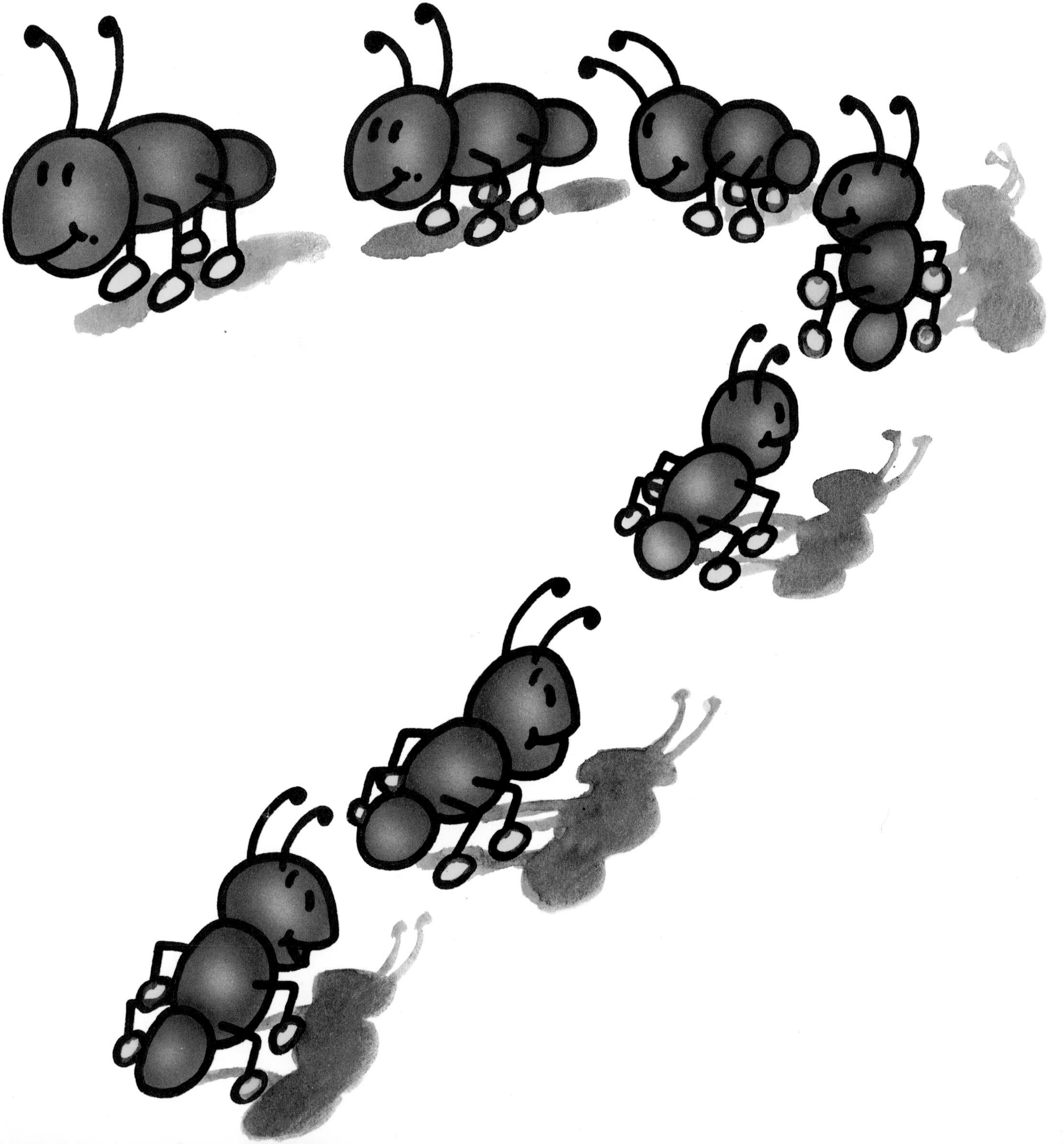

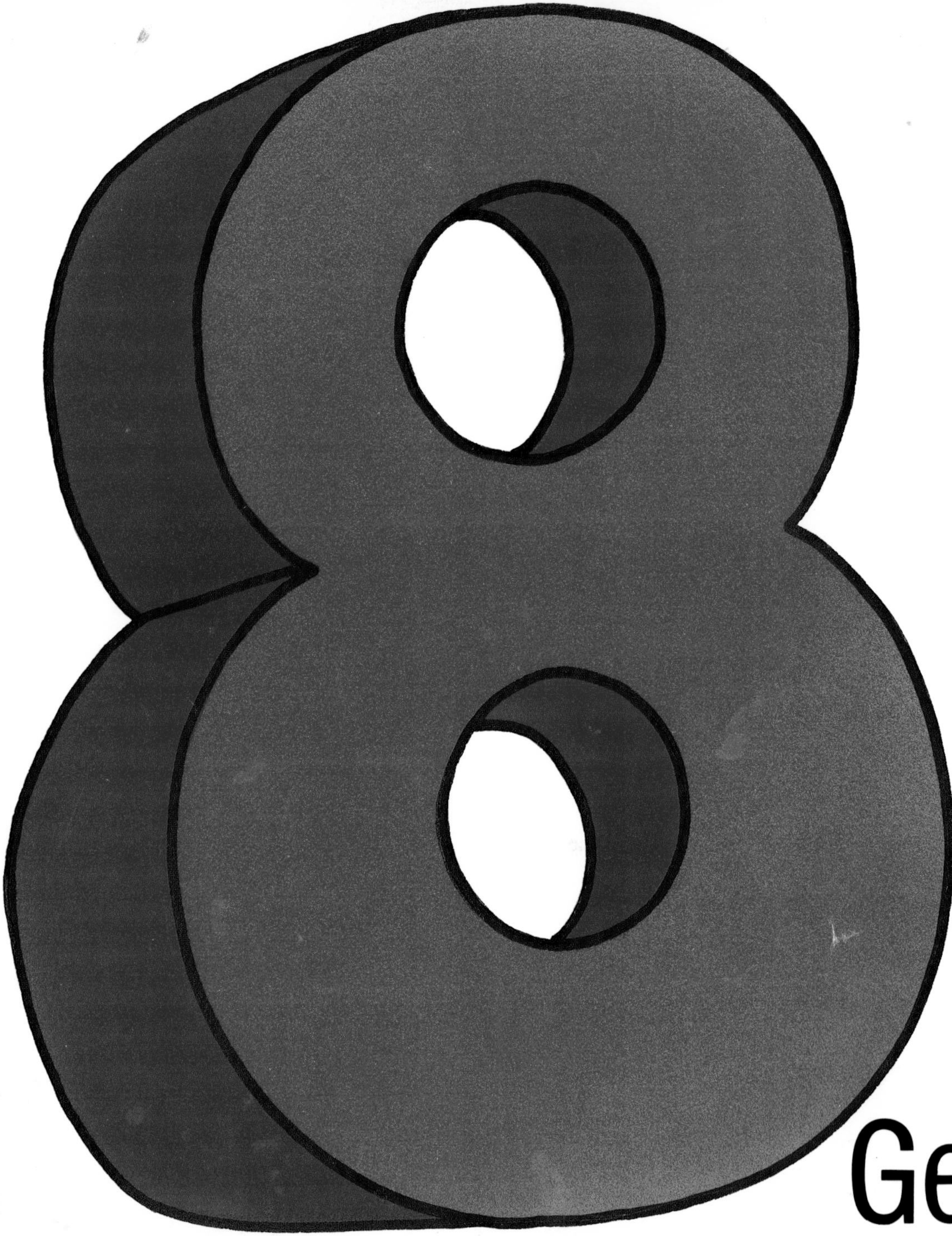

Geese

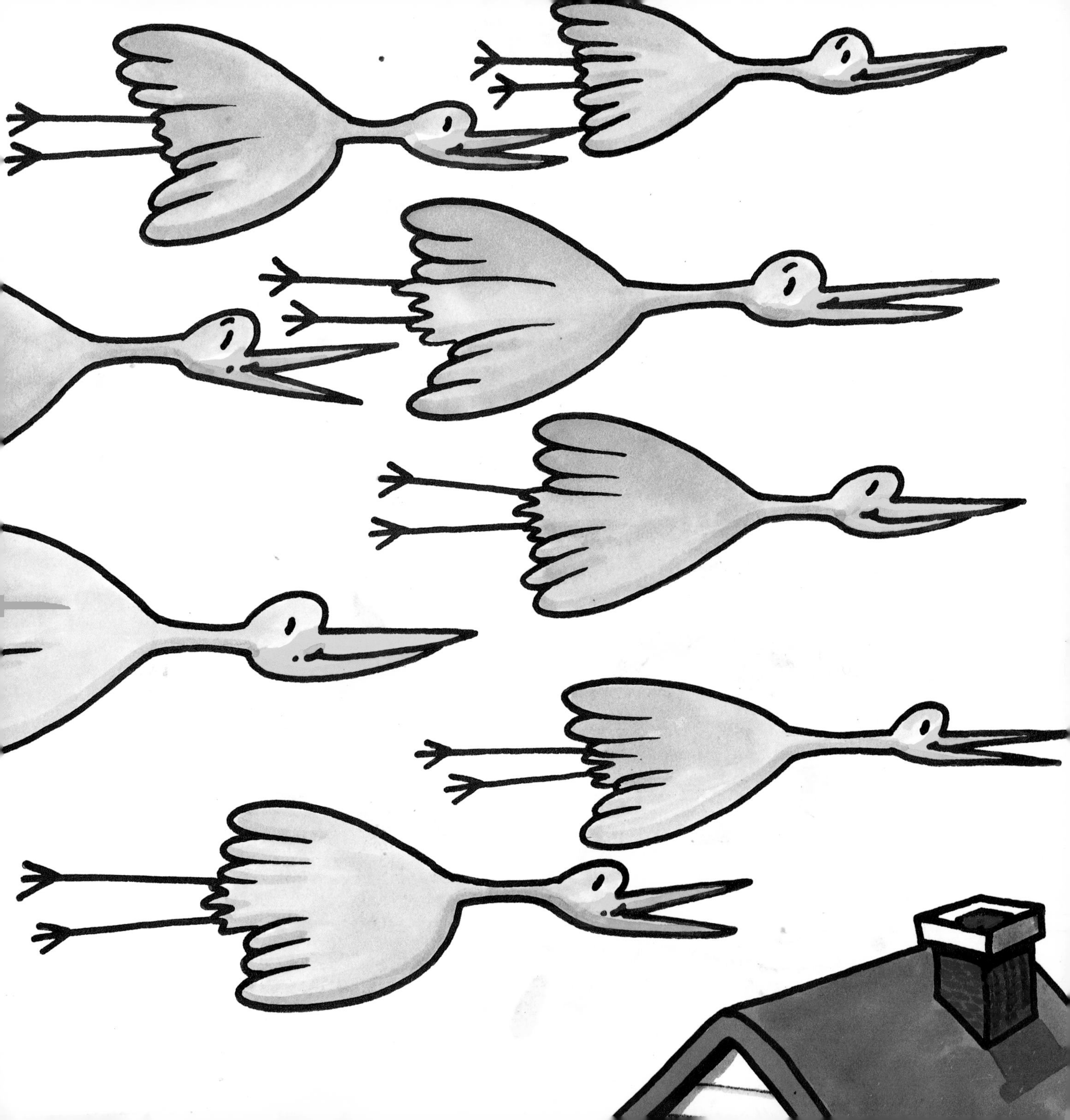

9

Monkeys

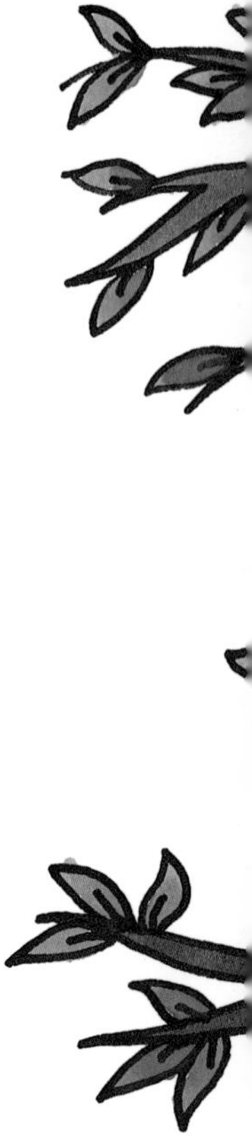

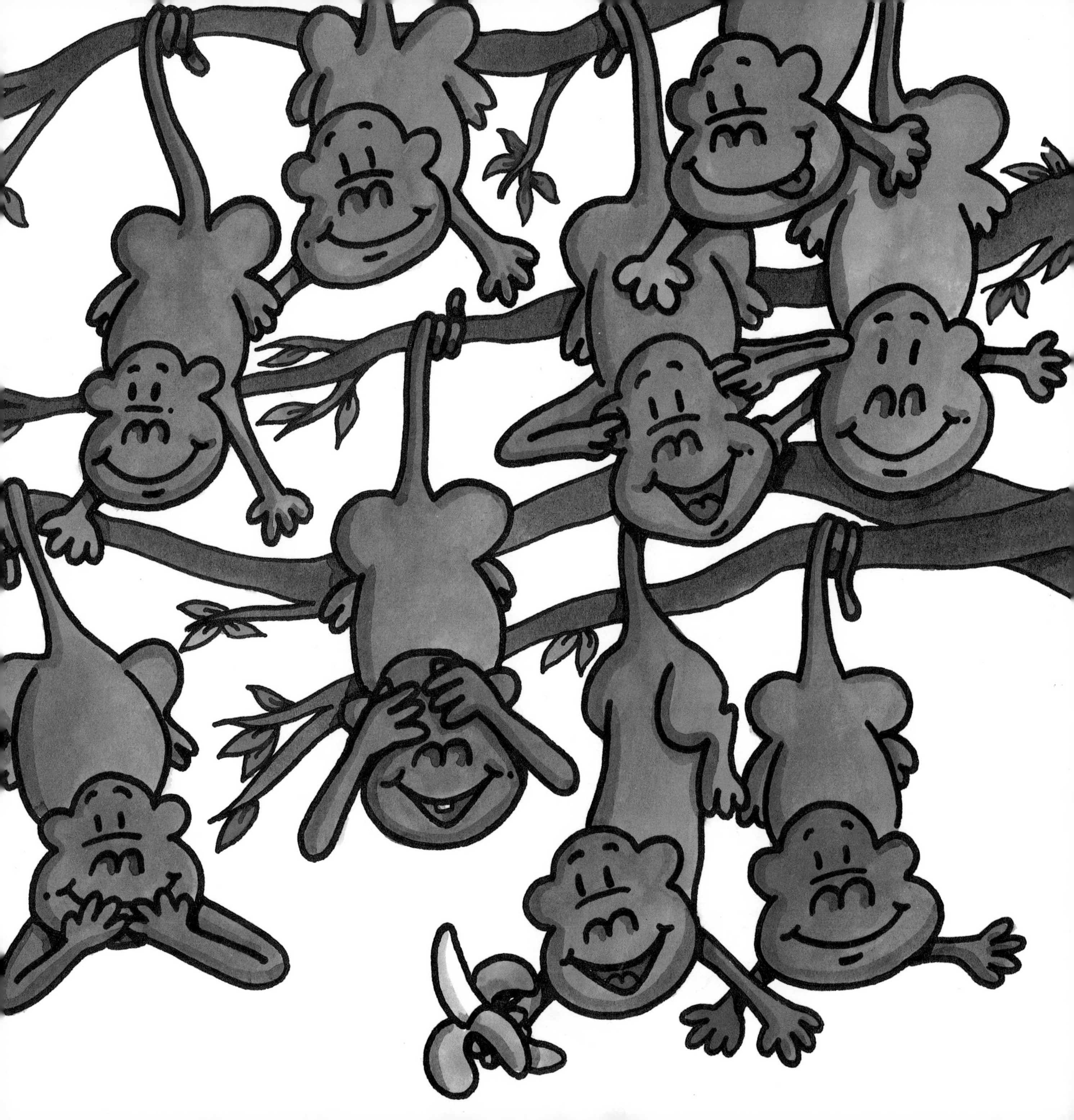

10

Prairie dogs

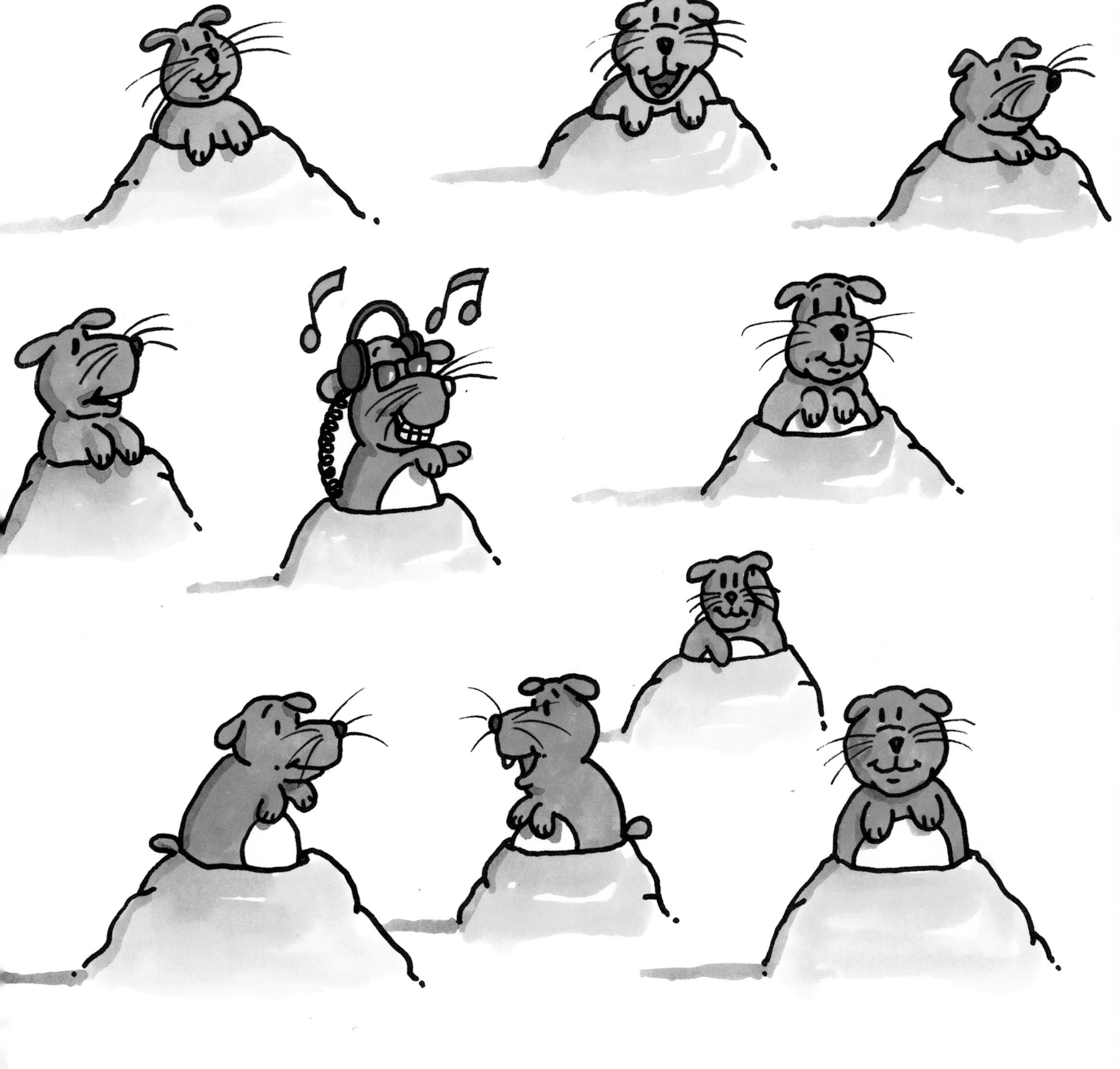

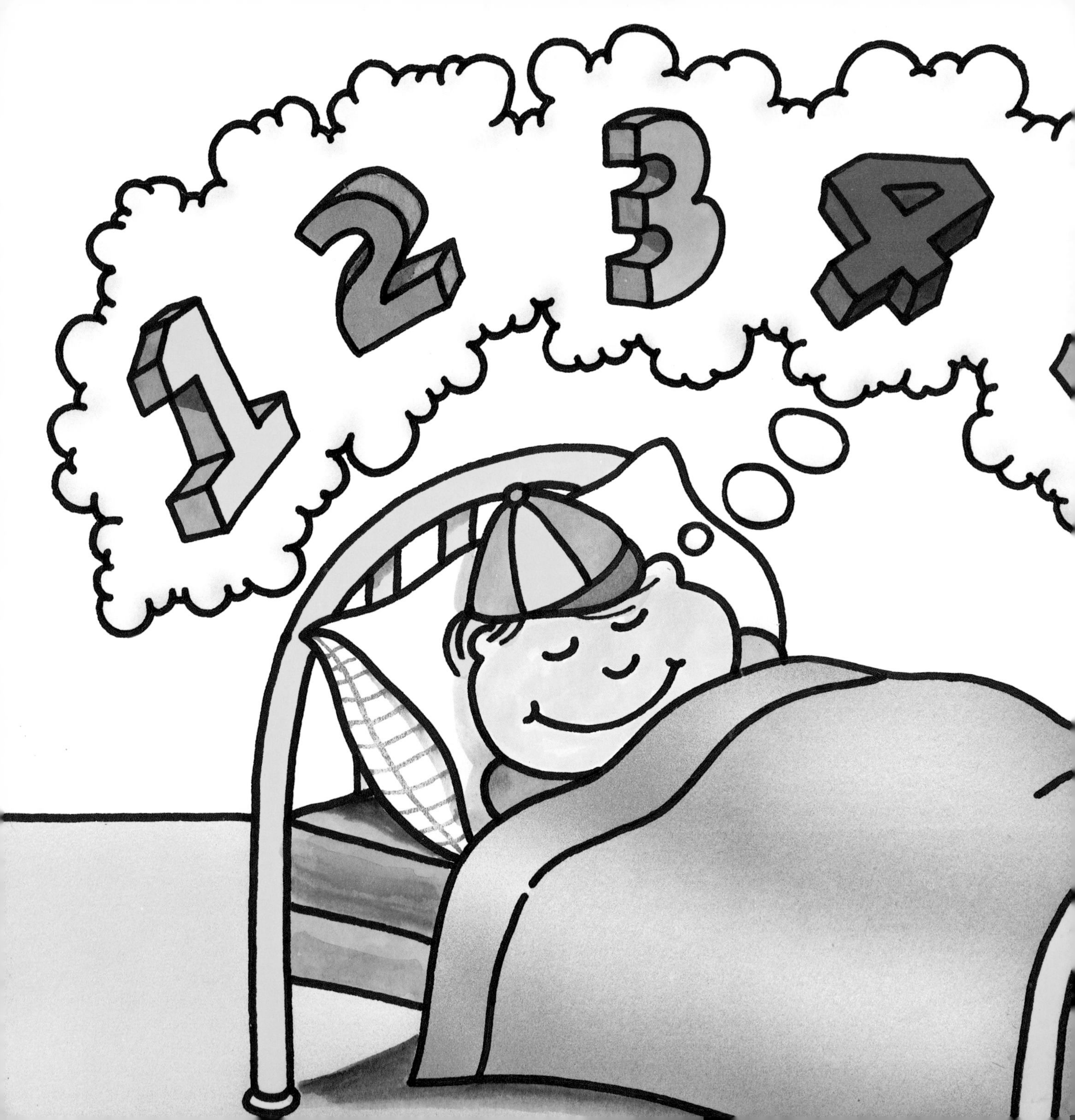
1 2 3 4

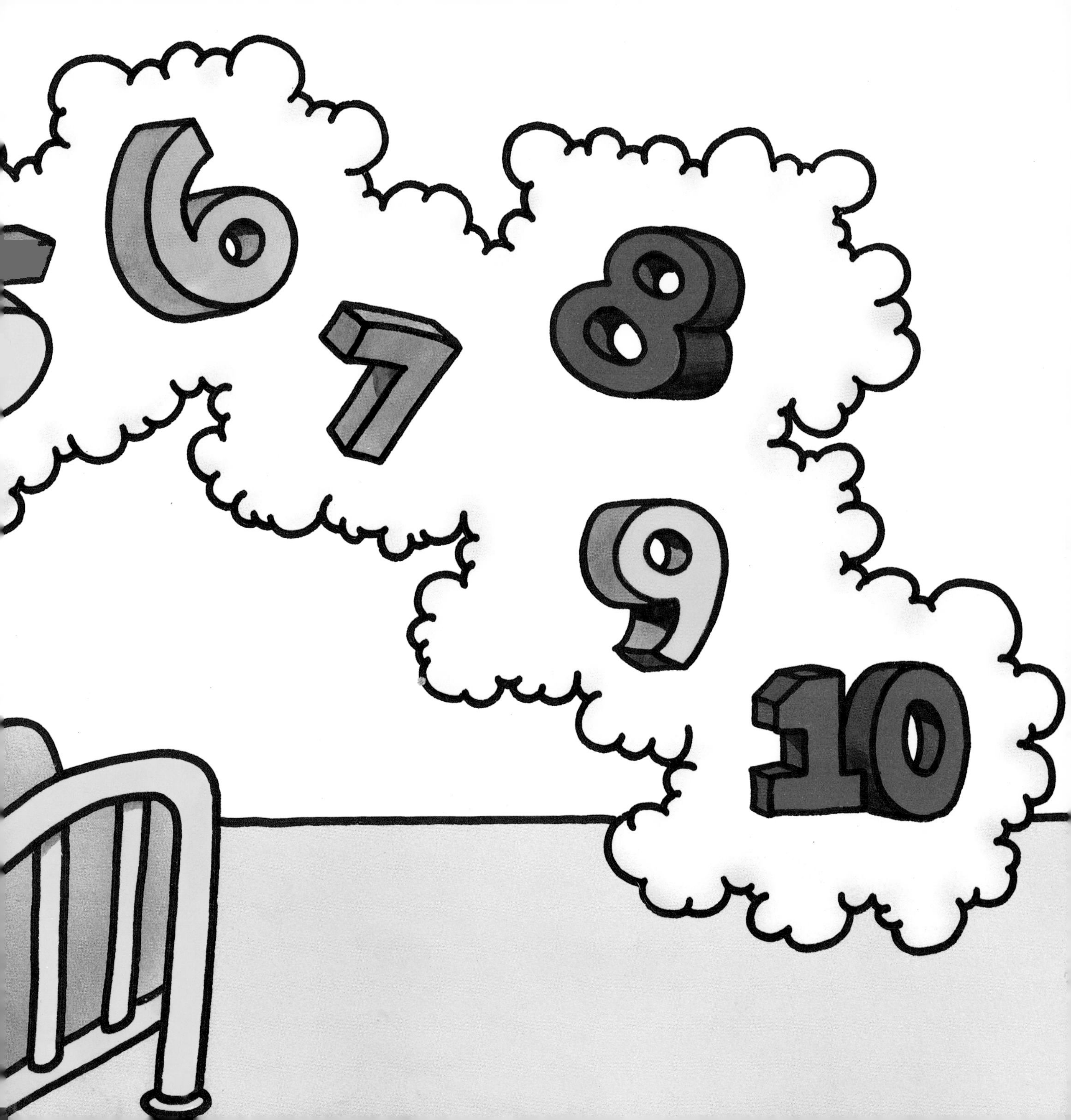
6
7
8
9
10

12

678